P9-CFB-172

GREAT MOMENTS IN SCIENCE

ISAAC NEWTON
DISCOVERS GRAVITY

by Douglas Hustad

Content Consultant
Waleed Meleis
Associate Professor
Electrical and Computer Engineering
Northeastern University

Core Library
An Imprint of Abdo Publishing
abdopublishing.com

abdopublishing.com

Published by Abdo Publishing, a division of ABDO, PO Box 398166, Minneapolis, Minnesota 55439. Copyright © 2016 by Abdo Consulting Group, Inc. International copyrights reserved in all countries. No part of this book may be reproduced in any form without written permission from the publisher. Core Library™ is a trademark and logo of Abdo Publishing.

Printed in the United States of America, North Mankato, Minnesota
082015
012016

THIS BOOK CONTAINS
RECYCLED MATERIALS

Cover Photo: Bettmann/Corbis/AP Images
Interior Photos: Bettmann/Corbis/AP Images, 1; Mary Evans/Science Source, 4, 45; Balazs Kovacs/iStockphoto, 8; NASA, 9 (bottom); Shutterstock Images, 9 (top left); iStockphoto, 9 (top right), 18; Ann Ronan Pictures/Print Collector/Getty Images, 12, 23; Marie-Lan Nguyen, 16; Hulton Archive/Getty Images, 20; Science Source, 25; SPL/Science Source, 28; BSIP/UIG/Getty Images, 32; Public Domain, 36; Red Line Editorial, 39

Editor: Arnold Ringstad
Series Designer: Maggie Villaume

Library of Congress Control Number: 2015945760

Cataloging-in-Publication Data
Hustad, Douglas.
 Isaac Newton discovers gravity / Douglas Hustad.
  p. cm. -- (Great moments in science)
 ISBN 978-1-68078-016-1 (lib. bdg.)
 Includes bibliographical references and index.
 1. Physicists--Great Britain--Juvenile literature. 2. Gravity--Juvenile literature.   I. Title.
 530--dc23

                                    2015945760

CONTENTS

ISAAC NEWTON AND THE APPLE

O n a late summer day in 1666, Isaac Newton was thinking in his garden. The 23-year-old was at his boyhood home of Woolsthorpe, in the east of England. Newton was spending time there while his studies at the University of Cambridge were interrupted. A plague had come to England in 1665. It was important to keep

An apple tree may have helped inspire Newton's work, which had a far-reaching impact on the study of gravity.

people apart so the disease could not spread. So the university closed. Newton went home.

On that summer day, he was thinking about gravity. He had been thinking about it for a while. The term *gravity* came from French and Latin. The French word *gravité* means "seriousness." The Latin word *gravitas* means "weight." But *gravity* was not used to describe a force of attraction until the 1640s. People had always known objects in the air fell to Earth. They did not know the reason. Newton wanted to learn more about this force.

Legend has it that on that day in 1666, Newton was literally struck with inspiration. As he sat in his garden, an apple fell from a tree onto his head. Suddenly, the attractive force all made sense to him. Although Newton was smart, it took more than one bonk on the head to develop his theories. But in stories Newton would later tell, an apple's fall was an important moment. He never actually mentioned it hitting him on the head, though.

From the Earth to the Moon

The apple helped Newton see the big picture. An apple falls to Earth rather than flying off. So gravity must reach the top of an apple tree. Newton reasoned that if it went that high, it must reach even farther than that. In fact, it must go all the way into space. Newton believed gravity was the force keeping the moon in place. He believed gravity controlled the entire universe.

Newton had studied the work of Galileo Galilei and René Descartes. Galileo was an Italian

PERSPECTIVE
Newton's Friend Remembers

William Stukeley was a longtime friend of Newton's. Later in Newton's life, Stukeley went to visit the aging scientist. They took a walk to Newton's garden. There, Newton said how the garden reminded him of his breakthrough long ago.

"He told me, he was just in the same situation, as when formerly, the notion of gravitation came into his mind. It was occasioned by the fall of an apple, as he sat in contemplative mood," Stukeley wrote.

Newton realized the same force that pulled apples to the ground also held the moon in place around Earth.

astronomer. Descartes was a French mathematician and philosopher. Both had died only a few decades earlier. Newton knew of their theories that an object in motion would stay in motion. Instead of continuing off into space, the moon stays around Earth. Gravity had to be the force that kept it in place.

Newton imagined the effect of gravity on a cannonball shot off a mountain. If you fired the

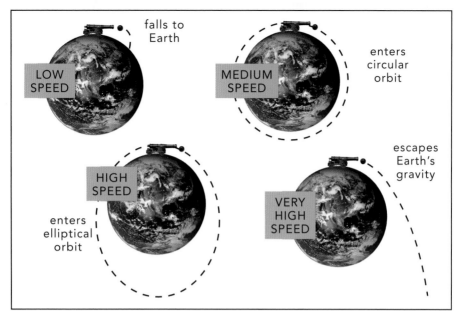

The Cannon Thought Experiment

The graphic above shows one of Newton's first thought experiments about gravity. If shot fast enough, a cannonball could be put into orbit around Earth. Do you think this idea expresses Newton's theory well? Is it easy to understand?

cannon, the cannonball would fly for a little while as it fell down to Earth. The faster you shot it, the farther it would go before hitting the ground. If you could somehow shoot it fast enough, it might never fall. It would continue circling the planet. This circle was known as an orbit.

Dueling Forces

On a small scale, Newton could not see that the force of gravity weakened as the distance between objects increased. Still, he reasoned that this must be the case. Otherwise, the moon would crash into Earth. All the planets would crash into the sun. The size of objects also seemed to affect the strength of gravity. Earth pulled on the apple, and the apple pulled on Earth. Earth was so much bigger that its force won out.

Newton searched for a way to calculate the exact force of gravity. But he could not get

The Real Tree

Newton never told anybody which tree produced the falling apple. But only one apple tree was on his farm at that time. Because of its significance, the tree has been cared for since the 1750s. It blew down in a storm in 1816 but was replanted. Despite being more than 350 years old, the tree grows at Woolsthorpe Manor today. It still produces apples, too. Several descendants made from the original tree are growing throughout England.

the calculations to work. He had theories about the force, but he could not prove them. So he set this work aside and went on to other studies. It would be another 20 years before he revisited gravity.

FURTHER EVIDENCE

Chapter One discusses the famous story of Isaac Newton, an apple, and the discovery of gravity. What is the main point of this chapter? What evidence supports its point? Read the article on the website below. Does the information on the website support the main evidence of the chapter? Does it introduce new evidence?

True or False?

mycorelibrary.com/gravity

CHAPTER TWO

THE YOUNG SCIENTIST

Isaac Newton was born on January 4, 1643, at his family's home in Woolsthorpe. His father, Isaac Sr., had died before Isaac was born. The Newtons were successful farmers. Isaac was expected to become a farmer himself.

Isaac was a small, sickly baby. It was reported he was born no bigger than a quart-sized pot. In 1646 his mother, Hannah, remarried and went to live with her

Newton's family wanted him to work on the family farm in Woolsthorpe.

new husband. Isaac's grandparents raised him until 1653. Then his stepfather died and his mother moved back to Woolsthorpe.

The Apprentice

While Isaac attended school, he needed a place to live. William Clarke and his family lived in town. They let Isaac stay in a room above their family's apothecary shop. Before pharmacies, people came to apothecaries for medicine. Clarke encouraged Isaac to help out around the shop. Isaac enjoyed learning about mixing medicines. He copied the recipes in his notebooks. Clarke was a thinker himself, and he had a large library. Isaac loved looking through these books. Isaac's time with the Clarkes influenced his later work.

Isaac began attending school in 1655. The school was several miles from home. It was too far to walk each day. So Isaac lived at the school. He was known as a quiet boy who rarely played with others. He was taught a lot of Latin but not much math. He only learned math that would be needed for farming.

Early Experiments

Isaac did not like to play sports, but he liked

outsmarting people. One day at school, some boys were seeing who could jump the farthest. Newton realized if he jumped when the wind blew hardest, he could win. He kept track of his jumps. He compared the distances in all wind conditions. With these figures, he came up with a way to measure the power of a storm.

From a young age, Isaac thought about the forces of the universe. The movement of stars and planets also interested him. He noticed the movement of the sun across the sky. He connected it with the time of day. He carved a sundial into a wall of the school, and people used it to tell time. They called it "Isaac's Dial."

At the time, not much was understood about the motion of the planets. The ancient Greek philosopher Aristotle had believed motion was a change in form. He believed the force that made things move was the same one that made people grow. René Descartes believed all space was filled with matter. He dismissed

As Newton read the works of older thinkers, including Aristotle, he began to challenge their views of the universe.

the notion of unseen forces acting on the planets. Isaac read these works. He formed his own ideas on force and motion.

Seeking the University

When Isaac was 15 years old, his mother called him back to Woolsthorpe. He was not yet done with school. But she believed he had all the education he needed to be a farmer. It was time for him to take up that responsibility. But farming was not a good fit for him. He did not enjoy it, and he was careless and forgetful. He would soon find a way out of farming.

Henry Stokes was the headmaster of Isaac's school. He also was a graduate of the University of Cambridge. He recognized Isaac's intelligence and tried to convince Hannah to send Isaac back to school. But Hannah wanted Isaac at home. At the time, having land and a farm was all that mattered.

PERSPECTIVES
The Philosopher on Gravity

Aristotle died in 322 BCE, but his ideas lived on into Newton's time. Aristotle did not understand much about the true nature of gravity. He believed everything was made up of four elements: air, fire, water, and earth. He thought air and fire rose above earth because they were lighter. An apple fell to the ground because it had the properties of water and earth. It was attracted to its natural spot among the elements. Many still believed this theory in Newton's time.

The University of Cambridge, one of England's best schools, was founded in the 1200s and is still running today.

So she asked her brother, William Ayscough, for help. Ayscough was an educated man who had graduated from Cambridge. Like Stokes, he believed young Isaac should continue his studies. Hannah finally agreed. She sent him back to classes. He finished school and soon was on his way to Cambridge.

Newton's friend William Stukeley described Newton's work building sundials. He explains Newton is not a sciolist, a person who simply pretends to be smart:

> *He spent a good deal of time, & art, in satisfying his curiosity this way; by making sun-dyals of divers forms, & constructions; every where about the house in every room, window; in his own bed chamber especially, in the yard, & entrys, wherever the sun came. He did not do it in a little manner, as minute sciolists would do, by making small sun-dyals: but show'd the greatness, & extent of his thought, by drawing long lines, tying long strings with running balls upon them; driving pegs into the walls, to mark hours, half hours & quarters. Many contriveances he used, to find out the periods, conversions, & elevations of that great luminary.*

Source: William Stukeley. "Memoirs of Sir Isaac Newton's Life." The Newton Project. University of Sussex, 2013. Web. July 1, 2015.

Point of View

The writer points out that Newton showed early signs of being a great scientist. What does he say those signs were? Read back through this chapter. Do you agree? Why or why not?

CHAPTER THREE

CAMBRIDGE AND DISCOVERING GRAVITY

Despite his intelligence, Newton entered Cambridge in 1661 with no special advantages. He received little money while at school. He had to pay his way by serving other students. He waited tables, shined shoes, and did other chores.

As in his earlier school, Newton spent a lot of time alone. Later in his college career, he visited a

Newton made amazing advances in science during his time at Cambridge.

tavern and played cards a few times. But mostly he stayed in and studied. Newton was assigned a tutor but rarely saw him. Newton largely taught himself.

The Old School

Cambridge was more than 400 years old by the time Newton attended. It remained a great university, but it was very old-fashioned. Many of the teachings relied on old ways of thinking. These ideas dated back to the Middle Ages or earlier.

A Cambridge education at that time relied on the ancient Greek philosopher Aristotle. Earth was seen as the center of the universe, and all the planets and stars revolved around it. People believed these objects moved on fixed rings.

But things were changing. People were challenging old ideas. Nicolaus Copernicus argued Earth revolved around the sun. Johannes Kepler believed planets orbited in oval shapes, rather than perfect circles. That suggested some kind of force must be acting on them.

Copernicus's idea that Earth revolved around the sun, rather than the other way around, was revolutionary.

In a notebook, Newton wrote, "Plato is my friend, Aristotle is my friend, but truth is my greater friend." Truth is what he would pursue.

Asking Questions

In Newton's first year, he filled a notebook with old beliefs. He then went through and wrote questions that challenged them. He called them "Certain Philosophical Questions." This would be Newton's standard scientific method. He would take what was known, then challenge it.

Newton did not believe Aristotle's view of matter. If Aristotle's belief in the four elements were not true, his theory about gravity was also untrue. An apple's "natural place" was not what caused it to fall.

Plague and Home Study

Immediately before Cambridge closed due to plague in 1665, Newton received his bachelor's degree. He then kept up his studies at home. He had mastered most of what was known about mathematics. But to define the force of gravity, he would need a way to work with curves. Calculations involving curved shapes were vital to understanding force and motion. Newton developed a new branch of mathematics called calculus. Its equations made it possible to make precise calculations involving curves.

Newton continued studying gravity. He tried to confirm his suspicion that the strength of gravity decreased with long distances. He realized gravity caused objects to accelerate. He decided to compare the acceleration of objects at different distances. This

Newton continued studying gravity, light, and other subjects while away from Cambridge.

would tell him whether the force was lessened at the longer distance.

Newton compared the moon to an apple falling on Earth. The distance to the moon was known. So was the time it took the moon to circle Earth. This allowed Newton to work out the moon's acceleration. He compared it to the apple's acceleration. He took into account the different distances from each object to the center of Earth.

From this work, Newton realized the force of gravity decreased as distance increased. The relationship between the two numbers follows the inverse square law. In other words, if the distance doubled, the force of gravity was reduced to one-fourth of the original value. If the distance tripled, the force was reduced to one-ninth.

Newton believed this law would be true not only for an apple and the moon but for the entire solar system. By discovering this law, Newton was discovering the underlying principles of gravity.

Other Experiments

Newton did not experiment with only gravity during this time. He also researched light and color. After buying a prism at a fair, he realized light was made of different colors. He reasoned the eye sees color based on what colors the object reflects. This research involved one highly dangerous experiment. He wished to see whether manipulating the eyeball would affect how humans see color. For this, Newton stuck a small knife between his eye and the bones of his face. Somehow he did no permanent damage.

CHAPTER FOUR

BECOMING A PROFESSOR

Newton tried to calculate the force of Earth acting on the moon. To do this, he needed to know Earth's diameter. But Earth's exact diameter was not exactly known at the time. The commonly accepted value was off by hundreds of miles. So the figures did not match up with his inverse square law. He was discouraged.

Newton's return to Cambridge brought more exciting discoveries.

He assumed some other force must be at work, and he went back to other studies.

Cambridge reopened in 1667, and Newton returned. He hoped to be chosen as a fellow, which would let him continue his work. If not, he would have to return to Woolsthorpe to farm or become a minister. He took the exams and was chosen. In 1668 he earned his master's degree.

By 1669 Newton's discoveries were beginning to be noticed. In particular, Professor Isaac Barrow at Cambridge began to take note of him. The two men had formed a close relationship. He encouraged Newton to share his findings. Newton had heard Barrow lecture as an undergraduate. This inspired his continued pursuits in mathematics. Barrow left Cambridge to take a position in the court of King Charles II. He recommended Newton take over for him.

Professorship and Getting Noticed

As a professor, Newton had to give lectures. Few students came to hear him, but this gave him more time for research. He studied light and color. He did more than only make theories. He invented a new kind of telescope. Newton boasted he had used it to clearly see Jupiter.

Newton lent the telescope to Barrow, who presented it to the Royal Society. The society was a club of famous and influential scientists in London, England. They were some of the leading thinkers at the time. The society was impressed

PERSPECTIVES
Isaac Barrow

When Isaac Barrow first met Newton, he was unimpressed. Newton spent little time with basic math. So when Barrow quizzed him on it, Newton nearly failed. But with time, he discovered the young man's talent. It was Barrow who encouraged Newton to share his research with the Royal Society. Newton took over Barrow's position at Cambridge only five years after nearly failing his exam.

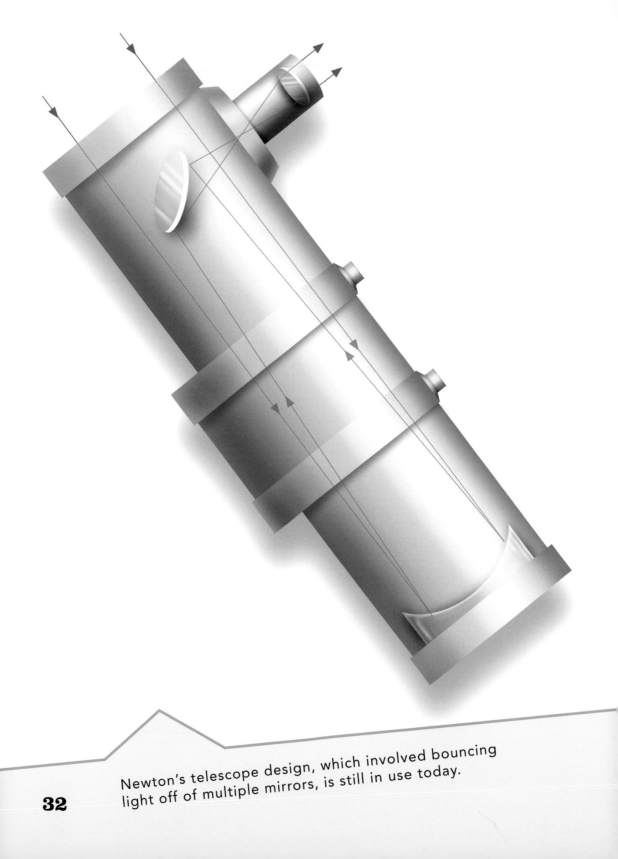

Newton's telescope design, which involved bouncing light off of multiple mirrors, is still in use today.

with Newton's telescope. They admitted him as a member in 1672.

The next decade or so saw Newton devote himself to light and telescope research. He also did research into alchemy. This field of study involves using chemistry to change materials into other materials. This research consumed much of Newton's life. Alchemy had little basis in science, but it did lead him to consider the nature of matter. And that would become important again very soon.

Revisiting Gravity

In 1684, at a coffee shop in London, three men were discussing the orbits of planets. They were Christopher Wren, Edmond Halley, and Robert Hooke. Halley wondered if the force of attraction between planets would decrease with distance. Hooke believed he had already proven that. But the others were skeptical. Wren bet 40 shillings that neither Hooke nor Halley could prove this theory. They had two months to do it.

Meeting Robert Hooke

Hooke was a member of the Royal Society. He first met Newton while studying light. Hooke had a brilliant mind himself. Perhaps because of this, the two immediately became rivals. Their rivalry continued for many years. It reached its peak when Newton published his laws on gravity. The two men wrote a series of letters to each other about their differing thoughts on gravity and other subjects.

Stumped, Halley went to see Newton. He was delighted when Newton told him he had solved that problem nearly 20 years ago. Newton went digging into his papers. He could not find his old work, but he promised to send it to Halley when it was ready.

Newton was always cautious before publishing anything. So he redid his calculations, made sure they worked, and sent them to Halley. Halley was thrilled. He rushed to show them to the Royal Society. Returning to his work on gravity inspired Newton. He began thinking more deeply about how the universe worked.

These two excerpts are from letters written by Isaac Barrow. He describes Newton and his work on optics:

> I send you the paper of my friend I promised, which I presume will give you much satisfaction; I pray having perused them so much as you think good, remand them to me; according to his desire, when I asked him the liberty to impart them to you. And I pray give me notice of your receiving them with your soonest convenience . . . because I am afraid of them; venturing them by post.
>
> His name is Mr. Newton; a fellow of our college & very young . . . but of an extraordinary genius & proficiency in these things.

Source: Joel Levy. Newton's Notebook. Hove, England: Quid Publishing, 2010. Print. 56–57.

Point of View

Take a close look at these passages. What is Barrow's opinion of Newton? What can you tell about their relationship from his letters?

PHILOSOPHIÆ

NATURALIS

PRINCIPIA

MATHEMATICA.

Autore *IS. NEWTON*, *Trin. Coll. Cantab. Soc.* Matheseos
Professore *Lucasiano*, & Societatis Regalis Sodali.

IMPRIMATUR·
S. PEPYS, *Reg. Soc.* PRÆSES.
Julii 5. 1686.

LONDINI,

Jussu *Societatis Regiæ* ac Typis *Josephi Streater.* Prostat apud
plures Bibliopolas. *Anno* MDCLXXXVII.

WRITING THE *PRINCIPIA*

Newton began putting together a new book. Its Latin title was *Philosophiæ Naturalis Principia Mathematica.* This means "Mathematical Principles of Natural Philosophy." It became known as the *Principia* for short. The first edition opened with a credit to Halley for encouraging Newton to publish it.

The *Principia* is among the most important books in the history of science.

The *Principia* had three parts, called books. Book I was an expanded version of what Newton had originally given to Halley. In this book, Newton wrote his three laws of motion. They built on the work of earlier thinkers, including Galileo. The first law stated an object in motion stays in motion unless an outside force acts on it. The second law stated the force of an object was equal to its mass multiplied by its acceleration. The third law stated for every action, there is an equal and opposite reaction. These simple laws controlled all motion in the universe.

PERSPECTIVES

Robert Hooke

Newton and Hooke were already rivals by the time the *Principia* was published. Hooke wanted credit for his role in the discovery of gravity. Hooke read an early draft of the book and demanded it not be published without this credit. Newton almost refused to publish the book because he was so insulted. The book was published, but Newton removed all references to any work Hooke did.

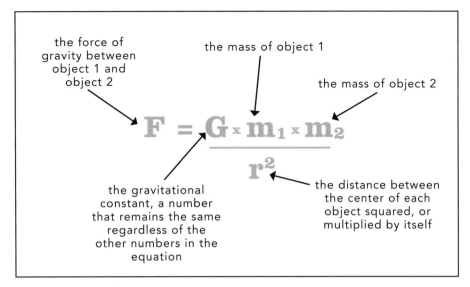

the force of gravity between object 1 and object 2

the mass of object 1

the mass of object 2

$$F = \frac{G \times m_1 \times m_2}{r^2}$$

the gravitational constant, a number that remains the same regardless of the other numbers in the equation

the distance between the center of each object squared, or multiplied by itself

Calculating Gravity

This is Newton's equation for figuring out the force of gravity, as described in the *Principia*. Each part of the equation is labeled and explained above. How does seeing the equation help you understand Newton's ideas about gravity? Does it help you better understand the inverse square law?

Newton also defined gravity in Book I. He used all the tools he had created over time to formally state this concept. His work in math and astronomy helped him develop the theory of gravity. Newton wrote that gravity is a force that attracts objects toward each other. Book II dealt mainly with fluids and the effect of friction.

Book III

In Book III Newton laid out his universal law of gravitation. He called this book the "System of the World." He was able to revisit his calculations from the plague years of 1665–1667. He now had more accurate data to use. He was able to prove the force of gravity on Earth was the same as the force that kept the moon in orbit.

Influence

The *Principia* was published in July 1687. It was instantly popular with other scientists and thinkers. Newton's laws became the way of the world.

Later Life

In his later years, Newton continued his research in all areas. He also continued to lecture at Cambridge. But he left the university in 1696 to work for Britain's National Mint. Newton oversaw the creation of new coins. He made sure they contained the right amount of metal. He also helped catch people who made fake coins. Newton held this position until he died in 1727. He was buried at Westminster Abbey in London. A carving on his tomb shows him studying among a pile of books.

Hundreds of years later, the famous physicist Albert Einstein revised Newton's findings. His theory of relativity showed that Newton's laws of motion were correct but incomplete. Newton's laws of motion became inaccurate as objects approached the speed of light. And Newton's law of gravitation broke down when gravity was very strong. But Einstein made one thing clear. He denied that he had in some way replaced Newton's research with his own: "Let no one suppose that the mighty work of Newton can really be superseded by this or any other theory."

EXPLORE ONLINE

Chapter Five talks about Newton's laws of motion and law of universal gravitation. The video at the website below demonstrates Newton's three laws of motion in the real world. Does the video answer any of the questions you had about Newton's laws?

Laws of Motion
mycorelibrary.com/gravity

IMPORTANT DATES

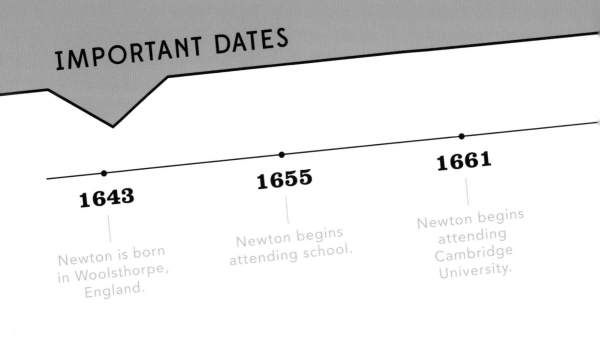

1643

Newton is born in Woolsthorpe, England.

1655

Newton begins attending school.

1661

Newton begins attending Cambridge University.

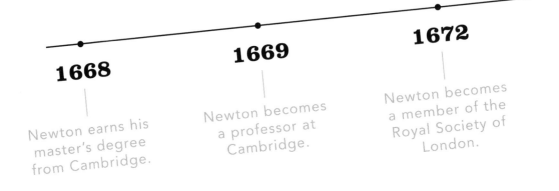

1668

Newton earns his master's degree from Cambridge.

1669

Newton becomes a professor at Cambridge.

1672

Newton becomes a member of the Royal Society of London.

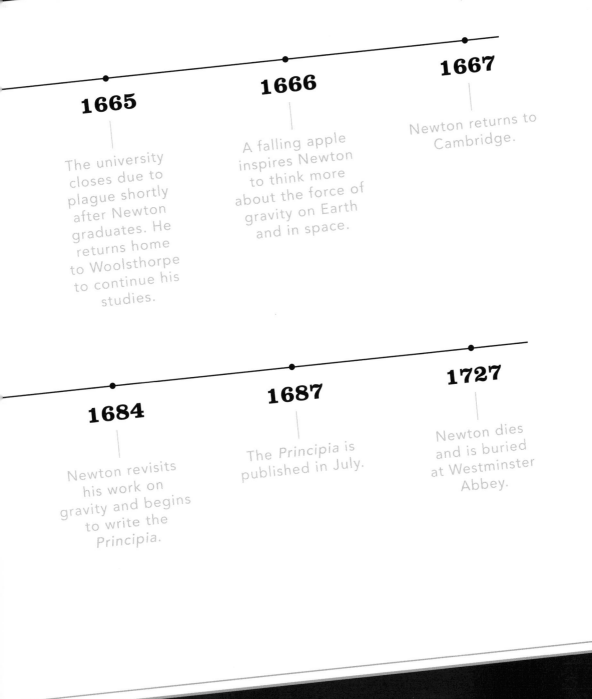

1665

The university closes due to plague shortly after Newton graduates. He returns home to Woolsthorpe to continue his studies.

1666

A falling apple inspires Newton to think more about the force of gravity on Earth and in space.

1667

Newton returns to Cambridge.

1684

Newton revisits his work on gravity and begins to write the *Principia*.

1687

The *Principia* is published in July.

1727

Newton dies and is buried at Westminster Abbey.

STOP AND THINK

Say What?

Reading about science and astronomy can mean learning a lot of new vocabulary. Find five words in this book you've never heard before. Use a dictionary to find out what they mean. Then write the meanings in your own words, and use each word in a sentence.

Take a Stand

Newton was not afraid to challenge old-fashioned thoughts on any subject. He did not always take what he read as the truth. He made experiments to see whether it was true. Do you think this is the best way to learn things? Or do you think reading an expert's opinion is just as good? Why?

Why Do I Care?

You might not think about gravity on a daily basis. It's just the way things are. What can you learn about the world by making observations? Have you ever seen something happen and wonder why it happened? How might you figure out the answer?

You Are There

Chapter Four discusses how Newton became a professor at Cambridge. Imagine you are a student there in the 1600s and hear him lecture. Write a letter home telling your friends what your experience was like. What qualities make him a good or a bad teacher? Be sure to add plenty of detail to your notes.

GLOSSARY

apothecary
an early type of pharmacy

calculus
a type of math dealing with curves and changes

diameter
the distance across something

fellow
a certain type of member of a society or organization

orbit
the curved path an object in space makes around another object in space

philosopher
somebody who makes observations and theories about questions of the universe

plague
a widespread disease

shilling
an old type of British currency used during Newton's life

undergraduate
a college student who has not yet earned a degree

LEARN MORE

Books

Chin, Jason. *Gravity*. New York: Roaring Brook Press, 2014.

Pascal, Janet. *Who Was Isaac Newton?* New York: Grosset & Dunlap, 2014.

Whiting, Jim. *Gravity*. Mankato, MN: Creative Education, 2013.

Websites

To learn more about Great Moments in Science, visit **booklinks.abdopublishing.com**. These links are routinely monitored and updated to provide the most current information available.

Visit **mycorelibrary.com** for free additional tools for teachers and students.

INDEX

ABOUT THE AUTHOR

Douglas Hustad is a children's author from Minnesota.